TO HEAR
HIS VOICE

TO HEAR HIS VOICE

Poem & Devotional Book

Catherine Posey

ROSE PETAL
PUBLISHING

To Hear His Voice
© 2020 by Catherine Posey

Published by Rose Petal Publishing
www.hearhisvoicepoetry.com

ISBN: 978-1-0878-9612-0 (softcover)
ISBN: 978-1-0878-9613-7 (hardcover)

All Scripture references taken from the King James Version. Public domain. All images are public domain or stock images.

_____

Front cover design by *Catherine Posey*
Back cover design by *Hannah Linder Designs*

To my Lord and Saviour, Jesus Christ,

for being so special to me.

CONTENTS

———◆———

Part 2: God's Plan for You

Part 3: All That He Has Done
(Your Notes)

My sheep hear my voice, and I know them,

and they follow me: John 10:27

TO HEAR HIS VOICE

Life is full of challenges,
troubles, heartaches, and fears—
but there is no reason for us to
endure bearing these burdens on
our own. Not only did Jesus Christ
die for our sins—so we may have
everlasting life with Him—but He
desires that we follow Him, so that
we can hear His voice when He
comforts, strengthens, and
guides. There is no greater
solace in the world—than
to hear His voice!

My sheep hear my voice, and I know them, and
they follow me: John 10:27

To Hear His Voice

When I fall down on my knees
Knowing my Shepherd's nearby
And tell Him all my heart and soul
He listens and draws me nigh

And when the hurt goes on to stay
And I do not understand
He takes His Word and comforts me
Then I fully trust in His plan

And when I'm down and can't get up
It is then He holds my all
Within His arms He carries me
Now I'm sheltered from a fall

When I think on these special things
That He does for me each day
I ponder the sweetest of them all
It's the whispers He doth say

For when I'm in His fold
Safe within His sight
It's His voice that I hear
And I know *all* will be right

What a special place to be in your life—alone, just you and your Lord. You utter to Him all your troubles, heartaches, or fears. He gently comes by and whispers sweet words of comfort, strength, or guidance. You hear His voice and you *know*. He, the Creator of all the universe, the Saviour of the world, the very One who died for you, has just talked to you.

This is a blessing that far too many Christians never experience. We can all have this sweet blessing, but we must extend beyond the comfort zone of our lives and reach deeper into being in His fold. A true walk with Him is knowing Him and Him knowing us, following Him, and then the sweetest blessing of all . . . hearing His voice.

Casting all your care upon him; for he careth for you. 1 Peter 5:7

He Careth for You

Whether vast or tiny
You see, it matters not
I know the One who cares
And I know He cares a lot

Small, insignificant things
Only meaningful to me
I take to the Lord in prayer
And I know He will see

Big mountains that I face
I never endure alone
When weary, long, and hard
Together we tread on

Many will carry burdens

So lonely and dismayed

Feeling quite strong enough

Yet sinking every day

So, when you need some care

From Someone who is true

Cast all your care on Him

For He careth for you

Sometimes there are small things in life that no one else would consider important, yet they mean something to us. We go to the Lord in prayer, and we wonder if our concern is too small to bring to God Almighty. We must realize how much He truly does care. His Word tells us that even the very hairs of our head are numbered (Luke 12:7). So, if He cares enough about us to know how many hairs we have, how much more He must care about every little thing that comes into our lives.

And when those mountains come and we feel that the load is too heavy to bear, He reaches down and carries us. How sweet to know that no matter what we are facing, whether big or small, the very One who made us *cares* as no one else can.

He maketh the storm a calm, so that the waves
thereof are still. Psalms 107:29

He Maketh the Storm a Calm

One by one they walk upon
The ship that sails the sea
Blue skies and birds that sing a song
A grand journey they hope will be

Yet as their voyage carries on
The wind and storm doth come
The waves will lift up high then low
Souls melt for what's to become

They strive with all their heart and soul
To row back to the shore
Try as they might they can't avail
Strength and hope are near no more

So, they cry unto their God above
They know He's the only One
Their trouble is too vast for them
There's nothing else that can be done

He hears their cry and knows their fear
So, He maketh the storm a calm
The waves gently lay back down
His touch is like a balm

So, when that storm that comes upon
Threatens to sink and pull you under
Cry out to Him with all your heart
For you see, there is No Other

We are going through life—enjoying each day and soaking in the sunshine—when suddenly a storm hits and takes our breath away. We feel overwhelmed, scared, tired, and confused—not knowing what to do.

It is at that moment, when we have reached the end of ourselves, that we should realize we need Him. If we continue trying to handle this storm on our own, we shall surely sink. Cry out to Him and tell Him your troubles and fears. For He maketh the storm a calm, so that the waves thereof are still.

He hath made every *thing* beautiful in his time:

Ecclesiastes 3:11

In His Time

We go to that quiet place
And seek the Lord in prayer
We bring to Him our desires
With hopes they'll soon be there

To hold a babe in arms
Or send a godly man
Right the hearts of loved ones
And help them take a stand

Then we watch for our answer
Expecting it to be soon
When there's delay in coming
Discouragement can lead to ruin

We can't always understand
His will or His chosen way
The path He sets before us
Fully meets the need for that day

His love for us is surpassing
A greater love you'll never find
He makes all things beautiful
But with God, it's in His time

We come to God with our requests, our desires, the things that we really want. Sometimes those things we ask for in prayer get answered right away. Other times, they do not. That's when we need to remember God loves us very much. His love for us is so great that He will ultimately only give us what He wants us to have when He knows the time is right.

For you see, God sees the whole picture, whereas we only see right now. He always knows exactly what is best for us. He answers our every prayer—though sometimes it is yes, sometimes it is no, and sometimes it is not yet. But one thing we can know—He hath made every thing beautiful in His time.

Create in me a clean heart, O God; and renew a
right spirit within me. Psalms 51:10

A Clean Heart, Oh God!

It has happened again
You have fallen once more
That sin that so besets you
You've sought forgiveness before

Or maybe this is a first
One you thought you'd never do
You can't believe you've caved
Into that sin so new to you

No matter new or old
That sin is just the same
It leaves you feeling dirty
Can't escape a heart of shame

It's peace and happiness you seek

For truly, don't we all

Sin will never bring you there

Just chains that bind for a fall

So how do we get victory

If giving in is all we've known

We must know in our heart

We cannot do it alone

Christ, He died for those sins

The victory has been won

Ask the Lord to create in you

A clean heart through His Son

It is here, there, everywhere—lurking around every corner. Sin and its never-ending temptations. So, how do we survive in this world without letting sin have the rule over our hearts and lives? There is but only one way—through Christ. He defeated sin and its hold on mankind. He won the victory on the cross. As a matter of fact, He paid for those very sins that so often burden us and bind us in chains. So why wouldn't He deliver us from sin's power over our lives? He will, but we have to be willing. Go to Him! Confess those sins to your Saviour, then ask Him to create a clean heart in you and to renew a right spirit within. He will!

Jesus Christ the same yesterday, and to day, and for ever. Hebrews 13:8

Yesterday, Today, and Forever

The mountains in their majesty
The ocean as it rages
The birds as they sing their songs
Unchanging over the ages

The flowers always blooming
We expect it every year
We can count on the trees to grow
It's the changing we all fear

Will this loved one live or die
Will I have the money I need
Will this illness change my life
Will my children hear my plea

This life can be so frightening

With changes we face each day

We must look to that very One

That's unchanging in every way

His Word and His sweet voice we hear

His love for whosoever

Jesus will always be the same

Yesterday, today, and forever

As we go through this life day by day, we face many different changes. There is precious little that actually stays the same. Just when we get comfortable with our present situation, another change comes, and we are left feeling uncertain and scared.

So, what a wonderful thing to have that special One in our lives that never changes—Jesus Christ. His love for us never changes. His Word never changes. His desire to be close to us never changes.

The truth that He died for our sins and has gone to prepare a place for us never changes. Jesus Christ is the Alpha, the Omega, the Beginning, the End, the Son of God, the King of Kings, and the Lord of Lords. He is our Comforter, our Guide, and our Strength. And He will never change! So, next time life throws you a whirlwind of unexpected change, remember this great truth and focus on the One who never changes!

Trust in the LORD with all thine heart; and lean not
unto thine own understanding. Proverbs 3:5

The Tomorrows Ahead

We have our thoughts
Of the way it should be
In our minds we know
What's right for me

We make our plans
And dreams for our life
Which way to go
To avoid any strife

But what we want
May not truly be
What God already knows
Is best for me

For we only see

What's here in the now

We can't know tomorrow

And so, we ask how

How can we know

How can we see

What's to become

Of my future and me

God sees them all

The tomorrows ahead

So, trust in Him fully

With your heart, not your head

So many things come upon us that we do not understand, and we fear what is going to happen. We do not know the future—the tomorrows that are ahead. We can only see our past and the now in our lives, therefore there is little we can do to comfort ourselves.

But God sees the whole picture. He can see our past, present, and every moment in our future. So, what we think is a wrong turn, God sees as necessary to keep us where He needs us to be, to protect us from harm, or to bring us back to Him. No matter how much we do not understand, we need to always trust God and believe with our whole heart that the very One who knows every detail of our future—is the very One in control!

He shall cover thee with his feathers, and under his wings shalt thou trust: Psalms 91:4

Under His Wings

I look back over the years
Of my life then and now
I see the ways You worked
The times I wondered how

How this problem would be solved
Oh, how would I get through
How could I find comfort
Which way, what do I do

Too weak to go much farther
No idea which way to go
No answer within reach
Raw pain within would flow

But just about the time

I came to the end of me

It's then You stretched Your wings

Covered and spoke, "I hold thee"

That's when You sent a verse

Or a message from Your man

Cared enough to give Your smile

Your direction and Your plan

You showed me the way to go

Put the answer in my sight

You gave me strength to go on

Not through me, but through Your might

Your feathers are so warm

Your comfort is so true

Under Your wings I will stay

You're my God and I love You

He *never* fails us. It's when we try to handle these troubles on our own that we simply get in the way. When we realize there is nothing we can do without Him, He can truly begin to do what He longs to do—cover us with His wings and comfort.

In the beginning God created the heaven and the earth. Genesis 1:1

I See God

When I look upon the beauty
That's before my eyes each day
I'm amazed at the wonders
I see God in every way

The stream that flows so lovely
The trees as they change in the fall
The mountains in their splendor
The uniqueness of us all

The ocean in its vastness
The array of flowers in fields
The precious smile of a baby
The beauty of rolling hills

The stars as they shine above

The fire as it crackles and soothes

The birds and their sweet melody

The sky's magnificent hues

In the beginning God created

Oh, how beautiful it is

If you open your eyes and see

You'll see God and all that's His

From the moment I awake, to the soft breathing of my slumber, everywhere I look—I see God. How can we not see God when we truly ponder the greatness of all His creation? Who but a Creator could cause one to shed tears when sad, relieving the pain? Who but a Creator could cause the decaying of leaves to bring about such a display of beautiful colors? Who but a Creator could cause the soothing sound of ocean waves, babbling brooks, and waterfalls to bring our hearts a feeling of sweet peace?

Who but a Creator could create a precious baby to be born out of the love of man and wife, all the while carrying on special traits and desires held by both parents?

These things have not come about by accident. They were designed by One much greater than we could ever imagine. These wonders were created for our enjoyment. So, when we look upon them, let us ponder . . . and see God!

I beseech you therefore, brethren, by the mercies of
God, that ye present your bodies a living sacrifice,
holy, acceptable unto God, *which* is your reasonable
service. And be not conformed to this world: but be
ye transformed by the renewing of your mind, that
ye may prove what *is* that good, and acceptable, and
perfect, will of God. Romans 12:1-2

His Will or Mine

The struggle is real
His will or mine
Which path to follow
My journey's fine

I want to go my way
I see across the fence
The grass is much greener
It makes so much sense

I jump right on over
Landing on both feet
I run toward the world
Pleasure I hope to meet

Is this side not greener

Why am I bound in chains

Will the world not help me

With bondage, sin, and pains

Reality sets in

The truth hits me hard

The grass is not greener

Now my life is marred

But then comes Jesus

Who says, "My way's best"

He gently heals my wounds

Gives my heart a rest

So, I give Him my all

Holding nothing back

Living sacrifice I'll be

No more a pit of black

There is no greater joy
Than to be within God's will
It's perfect and it's good
With a purpose to fulfill

The world is all about us, calling out our name, beckoning for us to chase down our own desires. We follow and leave the safety of His fold—His will. We are then left without the protection of the Shepherd. But if we come to Him as a living sacrifice, turn from the world, and renew our minds to be like Him, we can know the peace and joy of being in the center of God's perfect will!

Her children arise up, and call her blessed; her husband *also*, and he praiseth her. Proverbs 31:28

Blessed

Life has begun within
A mother you will be
You're overwhelmed with joy
This child soon you will see

Your tiny bundle greets you
Oh, what a precious sight
Amazing love has begun
Giving becomes a delight

You kiss their tears away
Tuck them in nice and warm
Hand in hand on a walk
Give comfort during a storm

You give a listening ear
They have troubles of their own
One day you wake and realize
That suddenly they've grown

What a special calling
To be blessed with a child
Raise them for His glory
God's looked on you and smiled

What an excitement it is to find out you are with child. The anticipation while waiting is exciting and wondrous. Once that precious baby arrives, there is nothing quite like that love that forms in your heart for your child. After years of sleepless nights, drying tears, fixing meals, folding laundry, and tucking in, you sometimes feel as if they will always be little.

But one day they will be grown, making a life of their own. Our job is not done. They still have that need to tell us their troubles or share an accomplishment, seeking a mother's praise. Of all these special things we get to do for our children, our greatest calling as a mother is to raise them to love and serve God. What an impact we can make on this world, by bringing up and leading to Christ another sweet child of His. What a blessed thing to be a mother. Let us not ever fall short of that great calling of God—to raise those precious children for Him.

In a moment, in the twinkling of an eye, at the last trump: for the trumpet shall sound, and the dead shall be raised incorruptible, and we shall be changed. 1 Corinthians 15:52

Twinkling of an Eye

Two women washing their clothes
Just talking about their day
Suddenly one disappears
No goodbye, just taken away

Man and wife driving down the road
She looks toward him and he's gone
The car crashes with no driver
The end has now had its dawn

Many souls all over the world
Abruptly vanish in thin air
Chaos and questions quickly rise
My baby, my loved one, just where

The Bible foretells of this day

Yet so many don't understand

In the twinkling of an eye

The saved will all leave this land

So, how can you prepare for this

What would God have you to do

Ask Jesus Christ to be your Saviour

Trusting His blood that was shed for you

So many are wandering through this life, focusing on their jobs, their finances, their entertainment, and their friends. Others are putting their focus on their families, working hard to provide, and spending time with those they love. All of these are not bad things, but rather are all good things. Yet, somehow while they are focusing on all these things that are in the today and the now, they are totally missing the importance of preparing for the future.

Our true purpose in life is to accept Jesus Christ

as our Saviour and to live for Him. That's when everything else will fall into place. He died for us so that we would not have to go to hell, but for those who ignore or reject his salvation, there will come a day when it is too late. Either death will steal them away and they will awake in the lake of fire, or Jesus Christ will come back in the Rapture of the Church and they will be left behind.

Don't be one of the millions who are left behind. Accept Jesus Christ as your own personal Saviour, because He died for you. Time is running out—He is coming soon!

Be still, and know that I *am* God:

Psalms 46:10

Be Still

Why, oh why, God
Has this happened to me
Be still, and know
That I am God

But, Lord, I can't
Go through this again
Be still, and know
That I am God

This request I've made
I need it to be
Be still, and know
That I am God

My heart is bleeding

Pain lies herein

Be still, and know

That I am God

For you see, He loves us

Too much to make mistakes

Be still and just listen

Trusting Him is what it takes

It has happened again. You are devastated, afraid, and overwhelmed. You come to God and ask, "Why, Lord?" We question Him. Why is He allowing this to happen? Why does He not stop the pain? Why won't He make this better? We don't understand. It is in those moments that we especially need to listen to His still small voice answering us, "Be still, and know that I am God."

God loves us too much to make any mistakes. He never promised to give us a life without pain, but He did promise to give us the strength to get through it. And all the while, He is walking right there by our side. Everything that happens is for a reason, and we need to trust God that He has it under control. So, when we are overwhelmed, full of pain, and question what is going on—we need to stop, be still, and know that *He is God!*

Now unto him that is able to do exceeding
abundantly above all that we ask or think,
Ephesians 3:20

Exceeding Abundantly

I pray that prayer once more
Beg God for my desire
As the door comes crashing closed
Discouragement I acquire

But then a new door opens
One I could have never found
I lean in to peek beyond
What I find brings hope unbound

A path that is much smoother
A love that's solid and true
Beauty beyond just seeing
Answers that only God knew

Each and every need I face

He supplies just in time

It's always exceedingly

Above what was in my mind

Because His ways are the best

Well beyond what we can do

We must trust Him with our life

Abundantly He gives to you

So many times in our own lives, we have prayed
for something specific, thinking we knew what the
answer was going to be. We already had our heart
fixed on it—then the door came crashing closed. But
that closed-door then led us to the door God actually
wanted us to walk through. Sometimes we must take
a journey that goes the long way around, in order to
get us exactly where He wants us to be. His paths are
always smoother. The special things He gives us are
always better than what we could have ever imagined

in our own mind that we need. Follow Him, hear His voice, because He is able to do exceeding abundantly above all that we ask or think. Just trust Him.

My sheep hear my voice, and I know them, and
they follow me: John 10:27

Follow Him

To follow Him
What does it mean
It means to obey
And keep ourselves clean

To read His Word
And take it to heart
Talk to Him daily
And never depart

Go to His Church
And learn about Him
Loving the brethren
Again and again

So, why should we

Do all these things

What is to gain

What will it bring

A heart of peace

Like you've never known

Strength to go on

Never being alone

Hearing His voice

When comfort He gives

The One who died

Knows us as He lives

His blessings are real

His love is so true

So, follow Him now

He'll take good care of you

If we truly want to hear Jesus Christ's voice when He speaks to us, we need to follow Him. If you have already accepted Jesus Christ as your Saviour, a good place to start would be reading your Bible, praying to Him every day, and attending a good, solid Bible-believing church faithfully.

This will bring you closer to the Saviour. He will then begin showing you what He wants for your life, how to obey His Word, and how to get victory over your sin—henceforth, truly following the Christ, the Son of God, the Saviour of the world, and your best friend!

And as *Jesus* passed by, he saw a man which was
blind from *his* birth. John 9:1

Jesus Passed By

In darkness he awoke
Blackness throughout his days
What hope could he have
When forced to begging ways

Been blind since his birth
Never seen a bird or tree
The one thing that he longed for
Sight, so he'd be free

Then one day he arose
As any other morn
To sit and beg for his food
As others looked with scorn

But then all had changed
The moment Jesus passed by
He spit upon the ground
Pressed the clay upon his eyes

He said to wash in the pool
And so he went his way
Did just as the Lord had said
Knowing he must obey

And suddenly he could see
The beauty of the land
New life for him had begun
Because of a healing hand

So, when Jesus passes by
Stops to speak His words to you
Do exactly as He says
His touch brings life anew

Countless people were lame, blind, filled with demons, or sick with other ailments. They had heard the word—there was a Man and He could heal. What it must have meant for that blind man when Jesus passed by. His whole life was changed in just a moment.

Just the same, our life is changed when Jesus touches our heart. When Jesus shows up to speak to us, we must listen very carefully and do exactly as He says. For when the Son of God passes by, our life will surely never be the same.

If we confess our sins, he is faithful and just to forgive us *our* sins, and to cleanse us from all unrighteousness. 1 John 1:9

Forgiven

I thank you, Lord
For all you've done
For being my Saviour
And God's perfect Son

For loving me
Through thick or thin
Forgiving me
Again and again

No matter how
Truly hard I try
I sin once more
I must know why

Why do you love
Why forgive me
Why show mercy
Help me to see

And then I saw
Your arms open wide
You on the cross
As you willingly died

You paid for those sins
Once and for all
I just need to confess
When to sin I fall

Your love is surpassing
This is the reason why
I'm just so thankful
Forgiven am I

It has happened again. You feel guilt, shame, and defeat. No matter who we are or how hard we try—we sin. But we have a merciful Father who loves us beyond our understanding. He wants us to tell Him all that we have done and ask Him for forgiveness. The amazing thing about this is—He forgives us when we ask! We must then ask Him for strength to not do it again, and then we need to forgive ourselves. Tomorrow is a new day with no mistakes in it.

I can do all things through Christ which
strengtheneth me. Philippians 4:13

All Things Through Christ

I just cannot do it
It's too hard, don't you see
It's beyond what I'm able
Don't expect it from me

I cannot give up this sin
I've enjoyed it for too long
Christ speaks and says I can
Giving strength to turn from wrong

What about this task I see
It's difficult for sure
Christ says He'll stand by my side
When vexed He'll help endure

This grief that I'm bearing

It's too heavy of a load

Christ says He will carry it

My burden on Him was bestowed

So you see, we must realize

Through Christ we can do *all things*

Just come to Him with all your heart

It's strength and comfort that He brings

Are you struggling? Feeling burdened down with a heavy load? Do you sometimes feel as if you cannot do what you need to do? When we are faced with these difficult things in life, how precious it is to realize that we do not have to go through them alone.

We *do not* have to carry our burdens by ourselves. We *do not* have to figure everything out. If we go to our Saviour Jesus Christ and ask Him, He will give us the strength we need. We *can* give up that besetting sin! We *can* accomplish that difficult task!

We *can* get through that burden or grief we are bearing! We can do *all things*–through Christ!

Pray without ceasing. 1 Thessalonians 5:17

Pray Without Ceasing

Our Saviour lives in our heart
He is there day and night
Longing for us to talk to Him
And love Him with all our might

He knows our every thought
And everything we do
He knows each tear that falls
And the sin our hearts pursue

So, why does the Lord want us
To tell Him all He knows
Just think how sad we would feel
If our loved ones' mouths stayed closed

This is a way to show our Lord

Our love for Him is great

Telling Him our heart and soul

A closeness we'll create

So, talk to Him throughout your day

Share all that is dear to you

Keeping a constant state of prayer

And you'll know a friend that's true

Just imagine if we lived with our spouse or our child, and we went through each day and never spoke a word to them. Would they feel loved? How important it is that we talk to those that we love. Jesus Christ is our Saviour, the One who died for us because He loves us so very much. So, how crucial it is that we talk to Him every day.

He wants us to tell Him what is on our heart—our troubles, our joys, and our needs. He wants us to thank Him for all that He has done and ask forgiveness for our sins. Be real with Him and talk to Him as you would a friend. Keep Him close to you throughout your day. Pray without ceasing—because you love Him!

Study to shew thyself approved unto God, a
workman that needeth not to be ashamed, rightly
dividing the word of truth. 2 Timothy 2:15

The Word of Truth

Oh, what could be quicker
Sharper than a two-edged sword
What could be more powerful
Than the mighty Word of the Lord

What could give more guidance
Or reproof that we need
Discern the intents of our heart
Than the Word of Truth we read

It's given by inspiration
Of the Almighty God above
A letter written just for us
Thus showing His great love

His Word has an answer

For every problem that we face

So why do we lay it down

Forgetting to run our race

We must turn to it every day

Embrace it in our heart

Mountains or valleys, come what may

From His Word we should never depart

We pray. We pour our hearts out to God. We beg Him to help us with our troubles. But do we hear what He is saying back to us? We *can* hear His words. We have the wonderful privilege to hold the very words of God in our hands! However, so many say that they struggle with understanding God's Word. If we have been saved, and we ask God to help us to understand—He will.

First Corinthians 2:10 says, *"But God hath revealed them unto us by his Spirit: for the Spirit searcheth all things, yea, the deep things of God."* God will help us as Christians to understand the deep things of God. The more we read the Bible, the more we will understand. Just don't lay it down. We have a race to run for Christ.

Verily I say unto you, Inasmuch as ye have done *it* unto one of the least of these my brethren, ye have done *it* unto me. Matthew 25:40

The Least of These

(Written at the age of 20 while serving in a church bus ministry in Chicago)

When I walk down the sidewalks

Of Chicago streets and roads

And I see the little children

In a house that's not a home

And I ask myself this question

Who will give a helping hand

If God's people do not reach them

Then who can

Then who will, who will see

Who will open up their eyes to these

Who will teach a little child

The way he should start

Make a difference, give some love

Change a heart

Who will wipe a dirty face

Who will catch a dropping tear

Who will feed them when they're hungry

Who will help them face their fears

We must tell them about Jesus

Of His grace and of His love

For there's no other answer

And He will

Then who will, who will care

Who will open up their heart and share

Who will teach a little child

The way he should start

Make a difference, give some love

Change a heart

So keep walking down those sidewalks

And be willing to give a hand

If God's people do not reach them

Then who can

When we give a part of our heart to a hurting child to show them love and kindness, we are showing Jesus Christ love and kindness. Oh, how many there are—scared, lonely, hungry, neglected, and sad children! Jesus said to forbid them not to come unto Him (Matthew 19:14). What a precious way for us to show our love for our Saviour—by loving His little children, the least of these.

O give thanks unto the LORD, for *he is* good: for
his mercy *endureth* for ever. Psalms 107:1

O Give Thanks

My eyes to see and ears to hear
My legs to walk upon
My arms to embrace and to love
My voice to sing a song

Soothing rivers and waterfalls
Mountains that tower above
Cool shade that the tree doth bring
The melody of a dove

Family to share our journey through
And friends that grow to care
Joyful tears from answered prayers
Knowing our God is there

A home that we can call our own

A bed for warmth and rest

Food to fill and meet our needs

Just feeling how much we are blessed

Salvation from the precious Christ

A gift only He could bring

Thus, a home waiting just for us

There's not a more beautiful thing

I ponder on these many things

It's all to Him I owe

O give thanks unto the Lord

He is good, His mercy doth show

We give a gift to someone we love. We wait and watch with excitement, hoping they will love it. They open up that gift and toss it aside. While this may be a bit of an exaggeration, do we do this to our Lord?

Do we go through this life, with all the many blessings God gives to us, and just toss them aside, never thanking Him or showing our gratitude? Do we stop and say "Thank you, Lord, for my family"? Do we consider that all that we have has been given to us by Him? O give thanks unto our great Lord, for truly, He *is* good!

The LORD *is* my rock, and my fortress, and my deliverer; my God, my strength, in whom I will trust; my buckler, and the horn of my salvation, *and* my high tower. Psalms 18:2

My Lord

To describe His infinite greatness
To tell you about my Lord
To share all He's done for us
Would take a lifetime and more

His love for man is surpassing
He died so we could be free
His power changes hearts and lives
It brings sinners to their knees

His strength is given when we are weak
He carries and comforts when low
His strong tower shelters in a storm
But you see, there's much more to know

In distress we cry and He listens

He delivers from turmoil within

There are so many things to say

So, with His names I will begin

He is the Alpha and Omega

The Beginning and the End

My Shepherd, my Saviour, my God

The Messiah that's my best friend

Wonderful, Counsellor, Lamb of God

Jesus Christ, God's only Son

The Way, the Truth, and the Life

The way to heaven, the only One

So, if He's not in your heart

The Prince of Peace and King of Kings

You're missing the true purpose of life

Salvation that only Christ brings

Jesus Christ, our Shepherd, the Lamb of God, our Saviour, and our best friend. He *is* everything we need. He is mighty and powerful. He has the power to save you and the power to change your life. Let God do His work through you.

Jesus saith unto him, I am the way, the truth, and the life: no man cometh unto the Father, but by me.

John 14:6

The Only Way

Do you know the Saviour
Have you been born again
Let's start at the beginning
Prepare you for the end

You must know you're a sinner
None is righteous, no not one
Our sin keeps us from heaven
But this story's not yet done

Jesus Christ died for those sins
The sins of all mankind
Yes, He knew your very name
Died for all your sins and mine

Then He was buried in the tomb
Rose again on the third day
The victory has been won
Under the blood our sins will stay

You must believe this in your heart
That He died, was buried, then rose
Then ask Him for forgiveness
To come in your heart and save your soul

It's really rather simple
Jesus is the only way
He truly wants to save you
So in heaven you'll be someday

SALVATION

I would like to ask you the most important question of your entire life: If you were to die today, do you *know* where you would spend eternity? Most people, when asked this question, would say, "I go to church," or "I have been a pretty good person," or "Nobody really can know for sure." But the Bible tells us we *can know* where we will spend eternity.

God's Word says to go to heaven we must be born again. In John 3:7 Jesus told Nicodemus, *"Ye must be born again."* The Bible gives us God's plan of how to be born again, which means to be saved. God's plan of salvation is simple.

WE ARE ALL SINNERS

As it is written, There is none righteous, no, not one:
Romans 3:10

For all have sinned, and come short of the glory of God;
Romans 3:23

God's Word tells us that because we are sinners, we fall short of His glory. In our natural state, none of us are pure enough to enter into heaven, because God cannot allow sin to enter in. Just one lie would be enough to keep us from entering heaven. James 2:10 says, *"For whosoever shall keep the whole law, and yet offend in one point, he is guilty of all."*

THERE IS A PENALTY FOR SIN

———❦———

For the wages of sin is death... Romans 6:23

...and all liars, shall have their part in the lake which burneth with fire and brimstone: which is the second death.
Revelation 21:8

And death and hell were cast into the lake of fire. This is the second death. And whosoever was not found written in the book of life was cast into the lake of fire.
Revelation 20:14-15

———❦———

In the Bible, we are told that because we are sinners we are condemned to death. This includes not only our physical death, but also eternal separation from God in hell.

WE HAVE A SUBSTITUTE WHO TOOK OUR DEATH PENALTY

But God commendeth his love toward us, in that, while we were yet sinners, Christ died for us. Romans 5:8

For the wages of sin is death; but the gift of God is eternal life through Jesus Christ our Lord. Romans 6:23

For God so loved the world, that he gave his only begotten Son, that whosoever believeth in him should not perish, but have everlasting life. John 3:16

Jesus Christ was mocked, spit upon, and cursed, then He died an agonizing death. While hanging on the old rugged cross, He knew your name and mine. He knew every sin we would ever commit. He could have called down ten thousand angels and ended His pain, but He willingly laid down His life for us. First John 3:16 says, "*Hereby perceive we the love of God, because he laid down his life for us:*"

He shed His precious blood so that *all* our sins would be paid for—past, present, and future. Our sins were laid on Him and He became our substitute. Why? Because He loves you and me.

Jesus died an agonizing death, but He did not stay in the grave. He rose three days later—conquering death, hell, and the grave.

WE CANNOT SAVE OURSELVES

For by grace are ye saved through faith; and that not of yourselves: it is the gift of God. Not of works, lest any man should boast. Ephesians 2:8-9

We can never be saved by being a good person or by going to church. Our works *do not* get us to heaven. We can only be saved by putting our faith and trust in Jesus Christ, God's Son, who died and paid for our sins on the cross.

Jesus saith unto him, I am the way, the truth, and the life: no man cometh unto the Father, but by me. John 14:6

ACCEPT JESUS CHRIST AS YOUR PERSONAL SAVIOUR

That if thou shalt confess with thy mouth the Lord Jesus, and shalt believe in thine heart that God hath raised him from the dead, thou shalt be saved. Romans 10:9

For whosoever shall call upon the name of the Lord shall be saved. Romans 10:13

You can come to Jesus right now and accept Him as your own personal Saviour. In your own words, pray something like this from your heart:

"Dear Lord Jesus, I know that I am a sinner. I know that I deserve hell. I believe that You died for me and that You were raised from the dead. Please forgive me for my sins and come into my heart and save me. I now completely trust You as my Saviour, to pay for my sins and keep me from going to hell. Thank you for dying for me. In Jesus' name, Amen."

There is nothing this world has to offer worth missing out on heaven. Every person will live throughout eternity in one of two places—heaven or hell. Please call upon Jesus to save you before it is eternally too late.

TRULY WALKING WITH GOD

—⟨✦⟩—

Once we have been saved and have accepted Jesus Christ as our Saviour, we can begin knowing Him personally. I would like to share some things we can do to grow closer to Him and know Him on a deeper level. The closer we draw to Him, the more we will hear His voice.

KEEP A CLEAN SLATE WITH GOD

If we confess our sins, he is faithful and just to forgive us our sins, and to cleanse us from all unrighteousness. 1 John 1:9

As soon as we know we have sinned, we should stop what we are doing and ask God to forgive us. If we have a sin that we continue struggling with, we must bring it to Him daily, asking for strength to overcome that sin that so easily besets us. He will give us strength. Christ died for those sins and He won the victory. As a saved child of God, we can live a victorious Christian life without sin having dominion over us. With every temptation, He will give us a way out—we just need to look.

There hath no temptation taken you but such as is common to man: but God is faithful, who will not suffer you to be tempted above that ye are able; but will with the temptation also make a way to escape, that ye may be able to bear it. 1 Corinthians 10:13

READ HIS WORD DAILY

Study to shew thyself approved unto God, a workman that needeth not to be ashamed, rightly dividing the word of truth. 2 Timothy 2:15

The Bible is more than just a book. It is God's love letter to us and a road map to life. His Word is full of amazing wisdom and truths, fascinating true stories, and God's promises. It foretells the things to come, and we have the honor of seeing prophecy being fulfilled.

What a privilege we have to be able to hold in our hands the very words of our great God. No matter how much we read, there is always something new for us in His Word. How important it is to read the Bible daily! The more we read, the closer we will be to Him.

A good place to start for a new believer would be the Gospel of John. Reading God's Word is the best way to hear His voice, because these are God's words that He has given just for us. Many times, He will speak directly to us concerning whatever situation we are currently in, giving the help that we need when we need it.

TALK TO HIM DAILY IN PRAYER

Pray without ceasing. 1 Thessalonians 5:17

Casting all your care upon him; for he careth for you.
1 Peter 5:7

He is our Saviour, the Son of God, the King of Kings, the Alpha and Omega, the Beginning and the End, *and* the Creator of the universe. He is our Good Shepherd and we get to talk to Him. Not only does He love us, but He cares about everything that we care about. We need to talk to Him, ask forgiveness for our sins, thank Him for what He has given us, tell Him our troubles, and then ask Him for those things that we need. When we pray to Him, we must always tell Him that we want His will to be done in our life and every situation. He sees the whole picture, whereas we only see the here and now.

ATTEND CHURCH FAITHFULLY

Not forsaking the assembling of ourselves together, as the manner of some is; but exhorting one another: and so much the more, as ye see the day approaching. Hebrews 10:25

Finding a good, solid Bible-believing church is very important. Here we can continually grow and learn more about our Saviour and His Word. We will have the blessing of having a church family—people who love us, care about us, and pray for us. While sitting under the preaching, we can receive messages straight from God, through the man of God. This is another special way that we can hear His voice. Also, we can be a blessing to others by showing our brethren love and praying for them. There are many ways in church that we can serve God and sing His praises.

TRUST GOD IN EVERYTHING

Trust in the LORD with all thine heart; and lean not unto thine own understanding. Proverbs 3:5

As we are building this strong walk with God through Bible reading, prayer, and church attendance, we need to start applying the truth of trusting God in our lives. It sounds like such a simple task, yet for so many, it is not so easily accomplished.

Truly trusting God in our lives means when things do not go our way, we trust God has a better plan. When the answer to our prayer is no, we know in our hearts that this is what God knows is best. When everything we know or understand is falling apart, we keep on trusting anyway—no matter what. He sees the whole picture, we do not. He is too wise to make any mistakes, and He loves us too much to hurt us unnecessarily. Trust Him.

And we know that all things work together for good to them that love God, to them who are the called according to his purpose. Romans 8:28

NEVER QUIT

For a just man falleth seven times, and riseth up again: but the wicked shall fall into mischief. Proverbs 24:16

Does this mean after we have been down and discouraged seven times and gotten back up to live for God, that we can then quit on God? No, it does not. It means a just man will not quit after falling, but will keep on living for God, no matter what life throws at him.

Don't quit. That is exactly what Satan would like to see you do. God will give you the victory over sin, and He will give you the strength to go on. Just keep walking with Him.

AUTHOR NOTES

My desire is that this poem and devotional book has been a blessing to you. If you have never been saved, my prayer is that you will accept Jesus Christ as your personal Saviour. If you have accepted Him and would like to share this with me, you can contact me through my website at hearhisvoicepoetry.com. I would love to hear your story. I pray that the words written within these pages would help another to open their heart and grow closer to Him in a way that they too can hear His voice.

At the back of this book, I have added a journal for you, *All That He Has Done.*

TIMES HE HAS SHOWN ME COMFORT

TIMES HE HAS GIVEN ME STRENGTH

TIMES HE HAS GUIDED ME

PRAYER REQUESTS

These pages are for your own notes. Start paying attention to those special whispers that God sends your way. Start watching for those special things He does. When He comforts you, write it down. When He gives you strength, write it down. When He gives you direction and guides you, write it down. It will become a treasure for you later to look back and remember all those special things He did–just for you!

We pray for things so many times, and when they get answered, we quickly forget. Writing down your prayer requests can be a big blessing, especially when we mark each one that God answers. As time goes on, what a blessing to look back and see *all that He has done.*

ABOUT THE AUTHOR

CATHERINE POSEY and her husband live in the country in the beautiful hills of West Virginia. They have five children and a border collie. She has been writing poetry since her childhood years and now enjoys writing for her Saviour. She also enjoys homeschooling her children, camping, and taking walks in nature.

HEARHISVOICEPOETRY.COM
FACEBOOK | HEARHISVOICEPOETRY

ALL THAT HE HAS DONE

Times He has shown me comfort

Times He has given me strength

Times He has guided me

PRAYER REQUESTS

Be careful for nothing; but in every thing by prayer and supplication with thanksgiving let your requests be made known unto God. Philippians 4:6

1._____

2._____

3._____

4._____

5._____

6._____

7._____

8._____

9._____

10._____

11._____

12._____

13._____

14._____

15._____

16._____

17._____

18._____

19._____

20._____

21._____

22._____

23._____

24._____

25._____

26._____

27._____

28._____

29._____

30._____

31._____

32._____

33._____

34._____

35._____

36._____

37._____

38._____

39._____

40._____

41._____

42._____

43._____

44._____

45._____

46._____

47._____

48._____

49._____

50._____

51._____

52._____

53._____

54._____

55._____

56._____

57._____

58._____

59._____

60._____

*In every thing give thanks: for this is the will of God in
Christ Jesus concerning you. 1 Thessalonians 5:18*

CPSIA information can be obtained
at www.ICGtesting.com
Printed in the USA
BVHW090756301120
594467BV00016B/754

9 781087 896120